FOREWORD

There is a large number of nonstate actors in the Western Hemisphere and around the world that exercise violence to advance their causes, radicalize the population, and move slowly but surely toward the achievement of their ideological and self-enrichment dreams. In Mexico, these nonstate actors have included a complex and enigmatic mix of transnational criminal organizations (TCOs) (cartels and mafia); enforcer gangs; political and ideological insurgents; and paramilitary "vigilante" organizations that generate violence and instability, erode democracy and the state, and challenge national security and sovereignty.

The author, Dr. Max Manwaring, explains that a new and dangerous dynamic has been inserted into the already crowded Mexican and Western Hemisphere security arena. That new dynamic is represented by a private military organization called the Zetas. Beginning in the early 1990s, the Zetas was organized and staffed by former members (deserters) from the Mexican Army's veteran elite Airborne Special Forces Group (GAFES). That private military organization now also includes former members from the formidable Guatemalan Kiabiles Special Forces organization. Thus, the Zeta is better trained, equipped, motivated, and experienced in irregular war than the Mexican police and army units that are supposed to control and subdue them. That new dynamic, as a consequence, employs an ambiguous mix of terrorism, crime, and conventional war tactics, operations, and strategies. This, in turn, generates relatively uncontrolled coercion and violence, and its perpetrators tend to create and consolidate semi-autonomous political enclaves (criminal free-states within the Mexican state) that develop into what the Mexican government has called

"Zones of Impunity." In such zones, criminal quasi states may operate in juxtaposition with the institutions of the weak *de jure* state, and force the local population to reconcile loyalties and adapt to an ambivalent and precarious existence that challenges traditional values as well as the law.

This volatile and dangerous security situation does not imply that Mexico is now a "failed state." Nevertheless, the threat exists and cannot be wished away. The purpose of this monograph, then, is to help political, military, policy, and opinion leaders think about explanations and responses that might apply to the unconventional, irregular, and ambiguous threats that privatized military violence generates. This monograph is also intended to help bring about a more relevant response to the strategic reality of the "Guerrillas Next Door" from the United States and the rest of the hemisphere. The author's analysis is cogent, and the Strategic Studies Institute is pleased to offer this monograph as a part of the ongoing dialogue on global land regional security and stability.

DOUGLAS C. LOVELACE, JR.
Director
Strategic Studies Institute

SUMMARY

A new and dangerous dynamic has been introduced into the Mexican internal security environment. That new dynamic involves the migration of power from traditional state and nonstate adversaries to nontraditional nonstate private military organizations such as the Zetas, enforcer gangs like the Aztecas, Negros, and Polones, and paramilitary triggermen. Moreover, the actions of these irregular nonstate actors tend to be more political-psychological than military, and further move the threat from hard power to soft power solutions.

In this connection, we examine the macro "what, why, who, how, and so what?" questions concerning the resultant type of conflict that has been and is being fought in Mexico. A useful way to organize these questions is to adopt a matrix approach. The matrix may be viewed as having four sets of elements: (1) **The Contextual Setting,** (the "what?" and beginning "why" questions); (2) **The Protagonist's Background, Organization, Operations, Motives, and Linkages** (the fundamental "who? why?" and "how" questions); (3) **The Strategic-Level Outcomes and Consequences** (the basic "so what?" question; and (4) **Recommendations** that address the salient implications. These various elements are mutually influencing and constitute the political-strategic level cause and effect dynamics of a given case.

The **Contextual Setting** explains that the irregular conflict phenomenon in Mexico is a response to historical socio-political factors, as well as new political-military dynamics being introduced into the internal security arena. New and fundamental change began to emerge in the 1980s. Mexico began to devolve from a strong, centralized, de facto unitary state that had the procedural features of democracy, but in which the ruling elites faced no scrutiny or accountability. At the same time, Mexico started to become a market state that responded to markets and profits rather than traditional government regulation. In that connection, we see the evolution of new private, nonstate, nontraditional warmaking entities (the Zetas, and others) capable of challenging the stability, security, and effective sovereignty of the nation-state. Thus, we see the erosion of democracy and the erosion of the state. In these terms, the internal security situation in Mexico is well beyond a simple law enforcement problem. It is also a socio-political problem, and a national security issue with implications beyond Mexico's borders.

The Protagonist's Background focuses on orientation and motivation. In this context, the Zeta is credited with the capability to sooner or later take control of the Gulf Cartel and expand operations into the territories of other cartels—and further challenge the sovereignty of the Mexican state. This cautionary tale of significant criminal-military challenge to effective sovereignty and traditional Mexican values takes us to the problem of response. The power to deal effectively with these kinds of threats is not hard military fire power or even more benign police power. Rather, an adequate response requires a "whole-of-government" approach that can apply the full human and physical resources of a nation and its international partners to achieve the individual and collective security and well-being that leads to societal peace and justice. This kind of conflict uses not only coercive military force, but also co-optive and coercive political and psychological persuasion. Combatants tend to be interspersed among ordinary people and have no permanent locations and no identity to differentiate them clearly from the rest of a given population. There is no secluded battlefield far away from population centers upon which armies can engage—armed engagements may take place anywhere. This type of conflict is not intended to destroy an enemy military force, but to capture the imaginations of people and the will of their leaders. Ultimately, the intent is to neutralize or control government and its traditional security forces so as to attain the level of freedom of movement and action that allows the achievement of desired enrichment.

Outcomes and Consequences illustrate where, in physical and value terms, contemporary criminal-military violence leads—and clearly answers the "so what?" question. In these terms, we take a close look at socio-political life in the State of Sinaloa. We center our attention on the reality of effective Mexican state sovereignty and the governing values being imposed in that "Zone of Impunity." The drug cartel, the enforcer gangs, and the Zetas operating in Sinaloa have marginalized Mexican state authority and replaced it with a criminal anarchy. That anarchy is defined by bribes, patronage, cronyism, violence, and personal whim. One is reminded of Thomas Hobbes description of life in a "State of Nature." That is, life is "nasty, brutish, and short."

Finally, trends and challenges and threats are identified that will have an impact on Mexico and its neighbors over the next several years. And, organizational and cognitive **Recommendations** are offered as a point of departure for possible responses.

A "NEW" DYNAMIC IN THE WESTERN HEMISPHERE SECURITY ENVIRONMENT: THE MEXICAN ZETAS AND OTHER PRIVATE ARMIES

Leftist insurgent groups such as Comandante Zero's Zapatista National Liberation Army (EZLN) are not the only nonstate political actors in Mexico or the Western Hemisphere that exercise violence to advertise their cause, radicalize the population, and move slowly but surely toward the achievement of their ideological and self-enrichment dreams.[1] But a new and dangerous dynamic has been introduced into the Mexican internal and the Western Hemisphere security environments. In Mexico, that new dynamic involves the migration of traditional hard-power national security and sovereignty threats from traditional state and nonstate adversaries to hard- and soft-power threats from small, nontraditional, private nonstate military organizations.[2] This "privatized violence" tends to include a complex and enigmatic mix of Transnational Criminal Organizations (TCOs) (cartels and mafia); small private military organizations such as the Zeta enforcer gangs (the Aztecas, Negros, and Polones); mercenary groups (the Central American Maras, Guatemalan Kaibiles, and paramilitary triggermen [*gatilleros*]); and other small paramilitary or vigilante organizations (hereafter cited as the gangs-TCO phenomenon).[3]

What makes these small private armies so effective is the absence of anyone to turn to for help. Weak and/or corrupt state security institutions, as in Mexico, are notoriously unhelpful and tend to be a part of the problem—not the solution. In such a vacuum, only a few relatively well-armed and disciplined individuals are capable of establishing their own rule of law. The dynamic of privatized violence (which has been on the global scene for centuries and is not really new) involves a powerful and ambiguous mix of terrorism, crime, and conventional war tactics and operations. This violence and its perpetrators tend to create and consolidate semiautonomous enclaves (criminal-free states) that develop into quasi states—and what the Mexican government calls "Zones of Impunity."[4] Leaders of these quasi-state (nonstate) political entities promulgate their own rule of law, negotiate alliances with traditional state and nonstate actors, and conduct an insurgency-type war against various state and nonstate adversaries. Additionally, criminal quasi-states may operate in juxtaposition with the institutions of weak de jure states and force the populations to adapt to an ambivalent and precarious existence that challenges traditional values as well as local law.[5]

The dynamics of privatized military force in Mexico signal two cogent trends. The first addresses the threat. It illustrates a "new" and unconventional battlefield that represents a nontraditional security threat to Mexico and its northern and southern neighbors. The second trend deals with response. These dynamics signal a new stability-security reality that is changing relations and roles among and between state security and service institutions. The "new" threat is not just a law enforcement problem, a national security issue, or even a social issue. It is much more, requiring a whole-of-government approach to dealing with the causes as well as the perpetrators of terrorism, criminality, and military violence. Ultimately, depending on response to threat, there is another signal that will define an underlying shift in state identity: a shift in state identity toward, or away from, some manifestation of state failure.

The mention of a possible shift in state identity here does not imply that Mexico is now a "failed state." That country has a vibrant middle class that supports law and order, and it has a relatively robust economy that can sustain a president willing to use the powers of the state to confront the gangs-TCO phenomenon. Under President Felipe Calderon, Mexico is responding constructively to the threat and can be seen as shifting away from the possibility of state failure.[6] Nevertheless, the threat exists; it is exacerbating the "new" privatized violence, and it cannot be wished away. As a consequence, this cautionary tale is intended to help political, military, policy, academic, and opinion leaders think strategically about explanations and responses that might apply to many of the unconventional, irregular, and ambiguous threats that Mexico and other countries face now and in the future. At the same time, this monograph is intended to help generate a more relevant response in the United States and the rest of the hemispheric community to the strategic reality of the "Guerrillas Next Door."[7]

In this connection, we examine the macro "what," "why," "who," "how," and "so what?" questions concerning the resultant type of conflict that has been and is being fought in Mexico. A useful way to organize these questions is to adopt a matrix approach. The matrix may be viewed as having four sets of elements: (1) **The Contextual Setting,** the "what" and the beginning "why" questions; (2) **The Protagonist's Background, Organization, Operations, Motives, and Linkages,** the fundamental "who," "why," and "how" questions; (3) **The Strategic-Level Outcomes and Consequences,** the basic "so what" questions; and (4) **Recommendations** that address the "so what" issues. These various elements are mutually influencing and constitute the political-strategic-level cause-and-effect dynamics of a given case. This approach is helpful and important in policy, practical, and theoretical terms.[8]

THE CONTEXTUAL SETTING

Two contextual themes are relevant to the analysis of Mexico's past, present, and future criminal and militarized violence. First, armed insurgent groups have arisen and prospered primarily as a response to historical sociopolitical factors. Yet the Mexican political structure has not developed programs and policies to remedy the societal ills that have generated and supported all these "revolutionary" movements.[9] Second, the continuing existence of political insurgents and armed criminal groups in Mexico "since forever" says much for their ability to adapt to and use the political system for their own purposes. This ability says much about both the motivational dedication of the insurgent-criminal leadership and the basic corruption within the postrevolutionary political system. Such corruption is likewise a result of long-standing political-historic factors, as well as new political-economic-social-military dynamics being introduced into the Mexican internal security situation.[10]

Historical-Political Context of Mexican Politics.

Many scholars agree that the key to understanding the contemporary Mexican political system lies in its origins in the social upheaval of the Revolution of 1910–20. The radical change precipitated by that event almost completely destroyed Mexico's past and forged a new and somewhat different nation. Some important old political habits did survive the revolution, however.[11]

Caudillismo (political control by "strong men") never has been very far under the surface of Mexican politics, and the constitution that emerged out of the Revolution did not promulgate the kind of democracy that liberals might champion. Thus, every president of Mexico since the Revolution has been a "great revolutionary leader" (*caudillo*), and the Mexican constitution is mostly an expression of hopes and wishes for future political, economic, and social justice. Accordingly, every president of the Republic represented historical continuity with the Revolution and defined the revolutionary goals that would be pursued during his 6-year term of office. And in true *caudillistic* fashion, the president provided justice. All actions of government—executive, legislative, and judicial—were taken in his name and were administered by his loyal political appointees.[12]

If the president was the leader (strong man) of the Revolution, the Institutional Revolutionary Party (PRI) was his functional representative. The PRI was the single, all-powerful mechanism of electoral activity, recruitment, and social control. Through the manipulation of the party mechanism and all its symbols during each 6-year term of presidential office, the political elites were able to maintain and enhance their power and wealth—and to enshrine Mexican personal freedom of political opinion, while systematically repressing political organizations that operated outside the limits allowed by the PRI.[13]

A New National Security Context.

With the malaise of corrupt caudillistic self-aggrandizement rooted at all levels of the Mexican political-economic-social system, forces for new and fundamental change began to emerge in the 1980s.

5

At that time, a set of economic measures designed to reduce inflation, control currency devaluation, and cut back on government spending led to bankruptcy in the business sector, increased unemployment, growing income inequality, and a much larger role for the private business sector in the government-controlled economy. Politically, the middle class, disaffected by public-sector inefficiencies generated by PRI corruption and resistance to serious reform — and declining living standards — began to abandon the PRI and vote for other party candidates for public office. As a consequence, Mexico began to devolve from a strong, centralized, de facto unitary state to what Professor (Ambassador) David C. Jordan calls an "anocratic" democracy. That is, Mexico is a state that has the procedural features of democracy but retains the characteristics of an autocracy, in which the ruling elites face no scrutiny or accountability.[14] At the same time, Mexico has become a market state that is moving toward "criminal free state" status. That is, Mexico is a state in which political power is migrating from the state to small, nonstate actors who organize into sprawling networks that maintain private armies, treasury and revenue sources, welfare services, and the ability both to make alliances with state and nonstate actors and to conduct war (the gang-TCO phenomenon).[15] This correlation of political, economic, and military forces, in turn, has generated an extremely volatile and dangerous internal security situation in Mexico that has been all but ignored in the United States.

The Anocratic Democracy. The policy-oriented definition of democracy that has been generally accepted and used in U.S. foreign policy over the past several years is best described as "procedural democracy." This definition tends to focus on the

6

election of civilian political leadership and, perhaps, on a relatively high level of participation on the part of the electorate. Thus, as long as a country is able to hold elections, it is considered a democracy—regardless of the level of accountability, transparency, resistance to corruption, and ability to extract and distribute resources for national development and the protection of human rights, liberties, and security.[16]

In contemporary Mexico, we observe important paradoxes in this concept of democracy. Elections are held on a regular basis, but leaders, candidates, and elected politicians are regularly assassinated; hundreds of government officials considered unacceptable to the armed nonstate actors have been assassinated following their elections. Additionally, intimidation, direct threats, kidnapping, and the use of relatively minor violence on a person and/or his family play an important role prior to elections. As a corollary, although the media institutions are free from state censorship, journalists, academicians, and folk musicians who make their anti-narco-gang opinion known too publicly are systematically assassinated.[17]

Consequently, it is hard to credit most Mexican elections as genuinely "democratic" or "free." Neither political party competition nor public participation in elections can be complete in an environment where violent and unscrupulous nonstate actors compete with legitimate political entities to control the government both before and after elections. Moreover, crediting Mexico as a democratic state is difficult as long as elected leaders are subject to corrupting control and intimidation or to informal vetoes imposed by criminal nonstate actors. Regardless of definitions, however, the persuasive and intimidating actions of the gang-TCO phenomenon in the Mexican electoral processes have pernicious effects on democracy and tend to erode the will and ability of the state to carry out its legitimizing functions.[18]

The Market State and the Gang-TCO Phenomenon. John Sullivan has identified an important shift in state form: from nation-state to market state and thereupon from market state to criminal-free state status. As the ability to wage war (conflict) devolves from traditional hierarchical state organizations to Internet-worked transnational nonstate actors, we can see the evolution of new warmaking entities (small private armies) capable of challenging the stability, security, and sovereignty of traditional nation-states. These private entities (terrorists, warlords, drug cartels, enforcer gangs, criminal gangs, and ethno-nationalistic extremists) respond to illicit market forces (such as illegal drugs, arms, and human trafficking) rather than the rule of law and are much more than "stateless" or nonstate groups. They are powerful organizations that not only can challenge the rule of law and the sovereignty of the nation-state but also are known to promulgate their own policy and laws—and impose their criminal values on societies or parts of societies (creating criminal-free zones and "badlands and bad neighborhoods" all around the world).[19]

In Mexico, as an unintended consequence of devolving political power from the state to private nonstate entities, we see not only the erosion of democracy but also the erosion of the state. Jordan argues that corruption at all levels is key to this problem and is a prime mover toward "narco-socialism."[20] Narco-politics has penetrated not only the executive, legislative, and judicial branches of the Mexican federal government but also state governments and municipalities.[21] The reality of corruption at any level

8

of government favoring the gang-TCO phenomenon mitigates against responsible governance and the public well-being. In these terms, the state's presence and authority is at best questionable in over more than 233 "Zones of Impunity" that exist throughout large geographical portions of Mexico. At the same time, the corruption reality brings into question the issue of effective state sovereignty. This is a feudal environment defined by extreme violence, patronage, bribes, kickbacks, cronyism, ethnic exclusion, and personal whim.[22]

Given the rise of the market state and violent privatized market-state actors, long-standing assumptions about national security and law enforcement are being challenged. Most notably, the ability (and power) to conduct conflict is moving from the traditional hierarchical nation-state to the privatized, horizontally-networked market state. Again, as noted above, that transition of power blurs the distinctions between and among crime, terrorism, and warfare.[23] At the same time, privatized violence is becoming (and in many regions has become) a feature of the transition to the market state and beyond. In this milieu, terrorists and organized crime come into conflict with warlords, insurgents, governments, private corporations, and nongovernmental organizations (NGOs). Any and all of these types of state and nonstate entities can hire and operate a small private army. In addition, all these entities can interact and blend or share attributes at given points in time. This is particularly relevant in the case of al-Qaeda *jihadi* terrorists operating in Spain, state-supported popular militias operating out of Venezuela, and nonstate criminal-political gangs operating in Colombia that seek to foment global, regional, and/or national or subnational instability, conflict, and political change. The linkage among war, terrorism, and crime is especially relevant in cases in which we see these types of actors making alliances with or declaring war against other similar privatized organizations, transnational criminal organizations, NGOs, and governments.

Typically, private armies and warlordism are the providence of failed or failing states. The common wisdom predicts that such states will eventually dissolve into nothing and provide no problems. Yet reality warns us that failed states do not simply go away. They normally devolve into international dependencies, people's democracies, narco-socialist states, criminal states, military dictatorships, or worse.[24]

The Resultant Internal Security Situation in Mexico. In the mid-1980s and later, a new political-economic force inserted itself into the changing internal security milieu. At a time when the political system was weakening and the economy privatizing, illicit drug trafficking started to become very big business. This is not to say that the illegal drug trafficking industry had theretofore not been operating in Mexico. It was. But in the 1990s, air and sea routes to the U.S. market from South America's "White Triangle" (main cocaine-producing regions in Colombia, Bolivia, and Peru) were being shut down. The narcotics-producing cartels, along with their TCO allies, began to use land routes through Central America and Mexico to transport their products to the U.S. market. As a consequence, between 60 and 90 percent of the illegal cocaine entering the United States is estimated to transit Central America and Mexico. Estimates of the money involved—in the billions of dollars—are mind-boggling.[25]

10

In this context, gangs and their TCO allies in Mexico, as in other countries, share many of the characteristics of a multinational Fortune 500 company. Thus, the phenomenon is reified in the form of an organization striving to make money, expand its markets, and move and act as freely as possible in the political jurisdictions within and between which it works. By performing its business tasks with super-efficiency and for maximum profit, the general organization employs its chief executive officers and boards of directors, councils, system of internal justice, lawyers, accountants, public affairs officers, negotiators, and franchised project managers. And, of course, this company has a security division, though somewhat more ruthless than one of a bona fide Fortune 500 corporation.[26]

Authorities have no consistent or reliable data on the gang-TCO phenomenon in Mexico. Nevertheless, the gang phenomenon in that country is acknowledged to be large and complex. In addition, the gang situation is known to be different in the north (along the U.S. border) than it is in the south (along the Guatemala-Belize borders). Second, the phenomenon is different in the areas between the northern and southern borders of Mexico. Third, a formidable gang presence is known to exist throughout the entire country (regardless of the accuracy of the data estimating the size and extent of this gang presence), and—given the weakness of national political-economic institutions—criminality has considerable opportunity to prosper.[27] As a result, the rate of homicides along the northern and southern borders is considered epidemic, and Mexico has the highest incidence of kidnapping in the world. Finally, violent gang and TCO activity in Mexico clearly threaten the socioeconomic and political development of the country.[28]

More specifically, the Central American Mara Salvatrucha 13 and Mara Salvatrucha 18 gangs (referred to collectively as the "Maras") have made significant inroads into Mexican territory and appear to be competing effectively with Mexican gangs. In the south—along the Belize-Guatemalan borders—the Maras have gained control of illegal immigrant and drug trafficking moving north through Mexico to the United States. The Central American Maras are also used as mercenaries by the northern drug cartels. Between the northern and southern borders, an ad hoc mix of up to 15,000 members of the Mexican gangs and Central American Maras are reported to be operating in more than 20 of Mexico's 30 states. Additionally, members and former members of the elite Guatemalan Special Forces (Kaibiles) are being recruited by the Gulf Cartel and the Zetas as mercenaries.[29]

The gangs operating on the northern border of Mexico are long-time, well-established, "generational" (that is, consisting of Mexican grandfathers, sons, and grandsons) organizations with 40-to-50-year histories. There are, reportedly, at least 24 different gangs operating in the city of Nuevo Laredo and 320 active gangs operating within the city of Juarez—with an estimated 17,000 members. The best-known gangs in the north are the Azteca, Mexicles, and Zeta organizations, whose members generally work as hired guns and drug runners for the major cartels operating the area. The major cartels include "the big four"—Juarez, Gulf, Sinaloa, and Tijuana cartels, which operate generally in the north. Despite the fact that most of the reported violence is concentrated in three northern states— Chihuahua, Sinaloa, and Baja California—the Juarez Cartel maintains a presence in 21 Mexican states; the Gulf Cartel is found in 13 states; the Sinaloa Cartel (see the later discussion of El Chapo) has located itself in 17

12

states; and remnants of the reportedly disintegrating Tijuana Cartel (Areliano Felix) are present in 15 states. There are also the Colima, Oaxaca, and Valencia cartels, which generally operate in the southern parts of Mexico. The Mexican Mafia (EME) further complicates the Mexican gang-TCO picture. At one time, all gangs operating south of Bakersfield, California, and into northern Mexico had to pay homage to and take orders from EME. That is no longer a rigid requirement, however; the Central American Maras are known to have broken that agreement as early as 2005.[30]

This convoluted array of gangs and TCOs — Central American Maras, Mexican Zetas, Guatemalan Kaibiles, Mexican drug cartels, and the Mexican Mafia — leaves an almost anarchical situation throughout Mexico. As each gang and TCO violently competes with others and within itself and works against the Mexican government to maximize market share and freedom of movement and action, we see a strategic internal security environment characterized by ambiguity, complexity, and unconventional (irregular) war. In addition, we see the slow erosion of the Mexican state and the establishment of small and large criminal-free enclaves in some of the cities and states of Mexico. Moreover, the spillover transcends the supposedly sovereign borders of Mexico and its neighbors (both south and north). This situation reminds one of the feudal medieval era. Violence and the fruits of violence — arbitrary and unprincipled political control — seem to be devolving to small, private, criminal nonstate actors. This is a serious challenge to democracy, stability, security, and sovereignty in Mexico and its neighbors.[31]

Conclusions.

The internal security environment that we see in Mexico today is dangerous and volatile. And it goes well beyond a simple law enforcement problem. Thus, the internal security situation is characterized by an unconventional battlefield which no one from the traditional-legal Westphalian school of conflict would recognize or be comfortable with. Instead of conventional, direct interstate war conducted by uniformed military forces of another country, we see something considerably more complex and ambiguous.

First, thanks to Steven Metz and Raymond Millen and their theory-building efforts, we see unconventional *non*state war, which tends to involve gangs, insurgents, drug traffickers, other TCOs, terrorists, and warlords who thrive in "ungoverned or weakly governed space" between and within various host countries. At the same time, we also see unconventional *intra*state war, which tends to involve direct and indirect conflict between state and nonstate actors.[32] Regardless of any given politically correct term for unconventional intrastate war, all state and nonstate actors involved in unconventional intrastate conflict are engaged in one common political act—war. That is, the goal is to control and/or radically change a government and to institutionalize the acceptance of the victor's will.[33] Additional strategic-level analytical commonalties in the contemporary battle space include the following:

- No formal declarations or terminations of war;
- No easily identified human foe to attack and defeat;
- No specific geographical territory to attack and

hold;
- No single credible government or political actor with which to deal; and,
- No guarantee that any agreement between or among contending actors will be honored.

Experience in unconventional nonstate and intrastate war further demonstrates that:
- There are no national or international laws, conventions, or treaties that cannot be ignored or utilized;
- There is no territory that cannot be bypassed or utilized;
- There are no national boundaries (frontiers) that cannot be bypassed or utilized; and,
- There are no instruments of power (military, diplomatic, economic, political, informational, or psychological) that can be ignored or left unused.

In these strategic-level terms, contemporary war (conflict) involves everyone, and the battlefield is everywhere. There are
- No front lines;
- No visible distinctions between civilian and irregular forces personnel; and,
- No sanctuaries.[34]

In this fragmented, complex, and ambiguous political-psychological violence–dominated environment, conflict must be considered and implemented as a whole. The power to deal with these kinds of situations is no longer hard combat firepower or even the more benign police power. Rather, power consists of the multilevel, combined political, psychological, moral, informational, economic, social, police, and military activity that can be brought to bear holistically on the causes and consequences — as well as the perpetrators — of violence.[35]

ZETAS: THE "WHO," "WHAT," AND "WHY" ARCHITECTURE

The "Who," "What," and "Why" case study methodological architecture focuses on protagonist leadership and organization, operations, motives, and linkages. Long-standing common wisdom has it that virtually any nonstate political actor with any kind of resolve can take advantage of the instability inherent in anything like the current Mexican internal security situation. The tendency is that the best-motivated and best-armed organization on the scene, or an alliance of these entities, will eventually control that instability for its own purposes. Carlos Marighella, in his well-known *Manual of the Urban Guerrilla*, elaborates on that wisdom: "A terrorist act is no different than any other urban guerrilla tactic, apart from the apparent facility with which it can be carried out. That will depend on planning and organization [and its resultant shock value]."[36] Thus, even though other privatized military organizations (including enforcer gangs) are operating in Mexico today, the Zetas appear to be the group most likely to be able to achieve their objectives. Zeta organization and planning has been outstanding, and the shock value of Zeta operations has been unequaled. Thus, as Marighella teaches, terrorism is a major force multiplier — "a weapon the revolution cannot do without."[37]

Background.

During the 80 years from 1920 through 2000 when Mexico was effectively a one-party unitary state controlled by the PRI, the drug cartels and the party made an accommodation. The question was, "Silver or lead?" Silver was a bribe; lead was a bullet to the head. The understanding that existed between the cartels and the party was that the political functionary would be better off to choose silver—simple as that! This does not mean that everyone was compromised, but it does mean that many party officials who were not compromised directly nevertheless chose not to see much that was going on. Vicente Fox's election to the Mexican presidency in 2000 broke the PRI's grip on Mexico and changed the status that allowed the cartels to go quietly about their business and share some of the wealth with their "friends." President Fox and later President Calderon became progressively more aggressive in confronting both the cartels and the police and the politicians whom the cartels had corrupted and co-opted. At about the same time, the flow of illegal narcotics through Mexico increased to the point such that drugs in Mexico are now estimated to produce $25 billion (in U.S. dollars) per year.[38]

Everything changed. The party and government were no longer as cooperative with the cartels as they had once been. The government was trying to exercise its traditional sovereignty over the Mexican national territory. The government, finding that to be more difficult than expected, recognized the possibility that the country might be moving toward "failed state status."[39] The various cartels were competing more violently than ever before. The cartels found themselves fighting with each other—and the government—for position in the new milieu. The profits to be had for the cartels, and the stakes for Mexico, were enormous. So, what is a businessman to do? Somehow, he must protect and enhance his resources, including trafficking routes and political and physical space from which to operate more freely, and he must simultaneously protect and expand his share of the market.

As a result of carefully watching the indicators noted above, the Gulf Cartel started to recruit members of the Mexican Army's elite Airborne Special Forces Group (GAFES) in the late 1990s. The GAFES members who defected to the Gulf Cartel called themselves Los Zetas. The intent of the cartel was to provide protection from government forces and other cartels, and the Gulf Cartel paid the Zetas salaries well beyond those paid by the army to make the effort worth their while. The idea proved to be a great success. Once the former soldiers were in place and functioning, their superior training, organization, equipment, experience, and discipline led them from simple protection missions to more challenging operations. The Zetas began to collect Gulf Cartel debts, secure new drug trafficking routes at the expense of other cartels, discourage defections from other parts of the cartel organization, and track down and execute particularly "worrysome" rival cartel and other gang leaders all over Mexico and Central America.[40] Subsequently, the Zetas expanded their activities to kidnapping, arms trafficking, money laundering, and creating their own routes to and from the United States, as well as developing their own access to cocaine sources in South America.[41] All this has been accomplished using the means delineated by Carlos Marighella, "often with grotesque savagery."[42]

The Zetas is the first private military organization in the Western Hemisphere to be made up of former military personnel from a regular army. Because of its considerable military expertise, previous experience in counterinsurgency combat, and guerrilla and urban warfare against leftist Mexican insurgent groups, the Zetas has made itself into a major private military-criminal organization in its own right. As a result, it has been labeled by Mexican scholar and TCO authority Raul Benetez as "the biggest, most serious threat to the nation's security."[43]

Organization and Operations.

Despite the lack of precise figures and specific and authoritative organizational charts, the Zetas appears to be much more than an ordinary enforcer gang organization working within a larger business model of a contemporary Mexican drug cartel. At first glance, there appears to be a hierarchical pyramid structure that is common among military organizations and some TCOs around the world.[44] A closer examination of the multilayered and networked structure, however, indicates a substantial corporate enterprise designed to conduct small and larger-scale business operations, along with terrorist, criminal, and military-type activities over large pieces of geographical territory and over time. As a result, the Zeta private military organization looks very much like any global business organization that can quickly, flexibly, and effectively respond to virtually any opportunity, challenge, or changing situation. As a consequence, there is probably more analytical utility in placing the traditional pyramid on its side and conceptualizing the Zeta organization as constituted by horizontal concentric circles.[45]

Organizational Structure. At the top, or at the center of the organizational structure, depending on whether one is looking at a pyramid or at concentric circles, is a small command structure. This group of senior individuals provides strategic- and operational-level guidance and support to its network of compartmentalized cells and to allied groups or associations. This structure allows relatively rapid shifting of operational control horizontally rather than through a relatively slow vertical military chain of command. Then, a second layer (circle) of leadership exists. These individuals oversee or manage guidance received from above, particularly in the areas of intelligence, operational planning, financial support, and recruitment and training. Additionally, this leadership group may manage special geographically and functionally distributed "project teams."[46]

At a third level, cell members may be involved in lower-level national and subnational, as well as international, activities of all kinds. The fourth and last level (circle) of the generalized and horizontalized organizational pyramid comprises a series of groups (*clickas*). These groups may be constituted by aspirants (that is, new recruits trying to prove themselves) and/ or by specialists. The specific subgroups include the following: (1) Los Halcones (The Hawks), who keep watch over distribution zones; (2) Las Ventanas (The Windows), who whistle or signal to warn of unexpected dangers in an operational area; 3) Los Manosos (The Cunning Ones), who acquire arms, ammunition, communications, and other military equipment; (4) Las Lepardas (The Leopards), who are, as prostitutes, attached to the intelligence section of the functional organization and are trained to extract information from their clients; and (5) Direccion (communications experts), who intercept phone calls, and follow and identify suspicious automobiles and persons, and have been known to engage in kidnapping and

20

executions.[47]

The Zetas' organizational structure strongly indicates that it is much more than an ordinary enforcer gang that is subordinate to a cartel's general structure. The Zetas has its own agenda and timetable and appears to be quite successful in achieving its short- and longer-term objectives. Militarily, and in the short term, the Zetas has developed an organizational structure and mystique that allows a relatively small force to accomplish the following objectives:

- Convince the people of a given area that the Zetas—not local politicians or local police, not federal authorities, and not other cartels—is the real power in that specific geographical terrain;
- Exert authority within its known area of operations, even if not physically present at a given moment;
- Fight both a larger force (such as police or the military or a rival gang) and another political actor at the same time.

Examples of terrorist means of convincing populations regarding prowess would include but not be limited to the following:

- November 2008–March 2009—several very senior police officials, including the commander of the federal police, were murdered in Mexico City.
- December 2008—severed heads of eight Mexican soldiers were found dumped in plastic bags near a shopping center in Chilpancingo, capital of the southern state of Guerrero.
- February 2009—another three severed heads were found in an icebox near Ciudad Juarez in

the northern state of Chihuahua.

- February 20, 2009—The chief of police for Ciudad Juarez, Roberto Orduna, resigned under pressure—after his deputy was murdered and it was revealed that another police officer would be killed every 48 hours until the chief (interestingly, a former army major) resigned. As the body count grew, Chief Orduna resigned and left the city.[48]

Over the longer term, the Zetas' first priority is to operate a successful business enterprise, with more than adequate self-protection and self-promotion. This private military organization encourages diversification of activities, diffusion of risk, and the flexibility to make quick adjustments, correct mistakes, and exploit developing opportunities. In that connection, the organization can deliberately expand or contract to adjust to specific requirements, and to new allies or enemies, while increasing profits. And, of course, this organization maintains a coherent mechanism for safeguarding operations at all levels and enforcing discipline throughout the structure. Consequently, over the past 10 or more years, the Zetas has slowly but surely moved from Gulf Cartel protection to developing drug trafficking routes of its own, to expanding from drug trafficking to arms and human trafficking and money laundering, and to an ambitious expansion policy into new territories and markets. In short, the Zetas appears to have taken over the main structure of the Gulf Cartel and launched an aggressive expansion strategy.[49]

Motives and Program of Action. The Mexican Zetas organization is credited with being self-reliant and self-contained. In addition to its own personnel, it has its own arms, communications, vehicles, and aircraft. The general reputation is one of high efficiency and absolute ruthlessness in pursuit of its territorial and commercial (self-enrichment) interests. As such, the Zetas is credited with the capability to sooner or later take over the Gulf Cartel and expand operations into the territories and markets of the other cartels. And as it progresses toward the control or incapacitation of rival organizations, it dominates territory, community life, and local and regional politics. Thus the explicit commercial motive is also implicitly and explicitly a political motive. Yet unlike some other enforcer gangs, TCOs, other private military organizations, insurgent groups, and neopopulists, the Zetas organization does not appear to be intent on completely destroying the traditional Mexican state political-economic-social system and replacing it with its own. Rather, the Zetas demonstrates a less radical option; it apparently seeks to incrementally "capture" the state.[50]

To accomplish this aim, the leaders of the Zetas have determined that—at a minimum—they need to be able to freely travel, communicate, and transfer funds all around the globe. For this, they need to be within easy reach of functioning population centers. Thus, the Zetas does not find the completely failed state particularly useful. It would prefer to have Mexico as a weak but moderately functional international entity. The shell of traditional state sovereignty protects the Zetas from outside (U.S.) intervention, but Mexican state weakness provides freedom to operate with impunity. And, importantly, although continued U.S. pressure will prevent Mexican authorities from abandoning the fight against illegal drug trafficking, there are many ways a functional state could exhibit a kind of cosmetic conformity while doing little in practice to undermine the power of the drug trafficking organizations.[51]

John Sullivan and Robert Bunker tell us exactly how the incremental capture of a state might conceivably take place. This pragmatic model of military and nonmilitary methods demonstrates the ways and means by which a transnational nonstate actor such as the Zetas can challenge and capture the de jure sovereignty of a given nation-state. This model has already proved to be the case in parts of Mexico, Central America, South America, and elsewhere in the world. This is how it works.

If an irregular attacker—criminal gangs, terrorists, insurgents, drug cartels, private military organizations, militant environmentalists, or a combination of the above—blends crime, terrorism, and war, he can extend his already significant influence. After embracing advanced technology, weaponry, including weapons of mass destruction (WMD) (including chemical and biological agents), radio frequency weapons, and advanced intelligence gathering technology, along with more common weapons systems, the attacker can transcend drug running, robbery, kidnapping, and murder and pose a significant challenge to the nation-state and its institutions.

Then, using complicity, intimidation, corruption, and indifference, the irregular attacker can quietly and subtly co-opt individual politicians and bureaucrats and gain political control of a given geographical or political enclave. Such corruption and distortion can potentially lead to the emergence of a network of government protection of illicit activities, and the emergence of a virtual criminal state or political entity. A series of networked enclaves could, then, become a dominant political actor within a state or group of states. Thus, rather than violently competing directly with a nation-state, an irregular attacker can criminally co-opt

24

and begin to seize control of the state indirectly.[52]

This model represents a triple threat to the authority and sovereignty of a government and those of its neighbors. First, murder, kidnapping, intimidation, corruption, and impunity from punishment undermine the ability and the will of the state to perform its legitimizing security and public service functions. Second, by violently imposing their power over bureaucrats and elected officials of the state, the TCOs and elements of the gang phenomenon compromise the exercise of state authority and replace it with their own. Third, by neutralizing (making irrelevant) government and taking control of portions of the national territory and performing some of the tasks of government, the gang phenomenon can de facto transform itself into quasi-states within a state. And the criminal leaders govern these areas as they wish.[53]

Conclusions.

As one watches TV and reads newspapers, the asymmetric Zeta challenge might appear to be ad hoc, without reason, and inordinately violent (terroristic). Nevertheless, a closer examination of organization and activities illustrates a slow but perceptible movement toward the capability to increase its freedom of movement and actions in Mexico, Central America, and elsewhere in the Western Hemisphere. After reviewing the basic facts of the brutal methods the Zetas use to insinuate their power over people, one can see that these seemingly random and senseless criminal acts have specific political-psychological objectives. After getting even closer to the situation, one can see that these objectives are not being lost on the intended audience.

Commercial enrichment seems to be the primary objective of gang-TCO phenomenon protagonists playing in the Mexican internal security arena. This is a serious challenge to existing law and order in Mexico and to the effective sovereignty of Mexico and the other nation-states within and between which the Zetas and other TCOs move. It is that, but it is also more. Sullivan warns us that resultant "para-states or criminal-free states fuel a bazaar of violence where [warlords, drug lords] and martial entrepreneurs fuel the convergence of crime and war."[54] At the same time, because political, military, and opinion leaders do not appear to understand how to deal with this ambiguous mix of intrastate violence, Peter Lupsha, a wise and long-time observer, argues that those leaders "are doing little more than watching, debating, and wrangling about how to deal with these seemingly unknown phenomena. As a consequence, territory, infrastructure, and stability are slowly destroyed, and thousands of innocents continue to die."[55]

OUTCOMES AND CONSEQUENCES: SOME CONTEMPORARY REALITY IN ONE DAY IN THE LIFE OF AN AMERICAN REPORTER SEEKING TO INTERVIEW A DRUG KINGPIN IN SINALOA

This vignette, taken from a very interesting and instructive article written by Guy Lawson,[56] is an attempt to capture the essence of the article. The intent here, however, is to briefly examine contemporary sociopolitical life in Sinaloa with a critical eye on the reality of effective state sovereignty.

The Individual Being Interviewed: Juaquin Guzman Loera, better known as "El Chapo" (Shorty).

El Chapo controls a Sinaloa Cartel that controls the Arizona border towns of Nogales and Mexicali. He has opposition, however. First, there are erstwhile friends who have developed a personal feud with El Chapo that seems to go on and on and become more and more violent. These antagonists are two brothers, Mochomo (Red Ant) and Barbas (the Beard), who are leaders of the Beltran Leyva cartel. Then there are the seemingly ever-present Zetas agents trying to expand their own and the Gulf Cartel's illegal drug routes into the United States. The Gulf Cartel and the Zetas appear to have teamed together with Mochomo and Barbas in an attempt to eliminate El Chapo from the market.

In the capital of the Mexican state of Sinaloa, Culiacan, El Chapo is known as "a kind of folk hero — part Robin Hood, part Billy the Kid." He has more money, more women, and more weapons than any other TCO in the area — except the Zetas. Because El Chapo is relatively generous with some (actually, very little) of his money, people "respect him." He grew up poor, planting corn and marijuana. Over time, he built massive underground tunnels to smuggle cocaine into Arizona, and he subsequently assembled a fleet of boats, trucks, and aircraft that made him one of the most wanted drug dealers in the world. And, he now — among other things — finances new entrepreneurs as they grow both marijuana and poppies for heroin. El Chapo, however, is most famous for his "miraculous escape" from a federal prison in 2001 just before he was to be extradited to the United States for trial on U.S. drug charges. "He had a plush suite in prison, complete with a personal chef, plenty of whisky, an endless supply of Viagra, and a girlfriend called Zulema." The common wisdom is that El Chapo gave all that up to go back to Sinaloa and help out his friends and neighbors.

Moreover, the people of Sinaloa are convinced that the federal government in Mexico City let El Chapo escape because he is the only drug lord who has the resources and intelligence to face up to the other cartels and to the Zetas.[57] The argument, simply put, is that the federal government cannot do much. The police are incompetent and corrupt; laws constrain government, while a TCO can do whatever it wants; and regular army troops are a poor match for the much better armed, equipped, and trained Zetas. In short, it is better to let the TCOs destroy themselves rather than fight them directly.

Principal Locations Where the Search for "Shorty" Took Place, and Some of the Topics of Conversation That Helped Pass the Time.

The State of Sinaloa, Mexico. Sinaloa is a small state on the Mexican Pacific coast across the Gulf of California from the Baja California peninsula. It is situated between the sea and the almost impassable Sierra Madre Occidental on the east. There are probably not many more than a million inhabitants of the entire state, but an average of three drug-related murders are estimated to take place every day of the year in Sinaloa. That statistic explains the front-page headline of the local newspaper on the day that our American reporter arrived in Culiacan: "Worse Than Iraq."

The Capital City of Culiacan, Sinaloa. That first day in Culiacan, everyone in the city was wondering what El Chapo might do to take revenge for the death of his 20-year-old son a few weeks earlier. The young man was shot and killed in broad daylight during a drive-by attack by 15 gunmen, one of whom fired a bazooka. The murder was attributed to the Beltran-Leyva cartel. Weeks later, four more decapitated bodies were dumped in the center of Culiacan with a note addressed to El Chapo, saying, "You're next." Three days later, three more bodies — this time with legs as well as heads severed — were found. Among them was a former police *comandante*. Within hours, another police officer was shot and killed, along with a companion and a bystander. Within another few days, two more grotesquely decapitated bodies were dumped outside a farm owned by a *capo* (criminal chieftain) allied with El Chapo.

That was just one series of events discussed on that first day in Culiacan. Something less important than the murder of El Chapo's son was also a topic of conversation. Only a few days before the arrival of our reporter, a gang of gunmen pulled up in front of an auto shop in the center of the city. They opened fire with AK-47s and AR-15s. Within minutes, nine people were dead. Then, as the assailants fled along Zapata Boulevard, they gunned down two police officers. On Insurgentes Avenue, the killers opened fire on federal troops stationed outside a judicial building. There was no pursuit and no arrests. All that anyone seemed to know was that the gunmen were after a small time *narcotraficante* known as "Alligator." A local official succinctly explained, "No one will talk."

As one might have guessed,

> Culiacan is a drug-industry town the way Los Angeles is an entertainment town. Every business is connected, directly or indirectly, with illegal drugs. There are narco discos and narco restaurants. In the upscale malls scattered around town, high-end jewelers sell gaudy

and expensive necklaces favored by narco wives, and girlfriends, and hookers. Narco chic is Valentino and Moschino pants, ostrich-skin boots, a black belt with a narco nickname (such as 'Alligator') engraved on it, and a Versace hand bag big enough to hold a stash of drugs and cash needed to pay off the police.

Thus, every day, Culiacan stages a sort of ongoing soap opera. But Culiacan is much smaller than Los Angeles. In Culiacan, one can see everyone and everything in one or two episodes.

On the Road and into Tamazula de Victoria. The American reporter was hoping to meet El Chapo and interview him. Through professional connections, he was introduced to "Julio," an opium (poppy) farmer, who considered himself a good friend of El Chapo. He has partied many times with El Chapo and his friends, and El Chapo supplies him with the seeds for the poppies he grows. Julio told the reporter that he could take him to a town called Tamazula where El Chapo lives — "if he isn't in Guatemala or El Salvador."

The highway inland and toward the mountains from Culiacan is dotted by large haciendas (ranches), sheltered behind 30-foot-high walls. Tamazula itself boasts a new school and condo developments — signs of the prosperity bought with narco dollars. In the middle of the village, on a hill overlooking the valley, a mansion stands behind large black steel gates. "At the bottom of the hill, just under the gaze of the narco mansion, there is a kind of contradiction common in the Sierra Madres. It is an army outpost ironically illustrating that the fortunes of the law and outlaws are inextricably entwined." Julio explained that the house belongs to one of El Chapo's allies. But El Chapo is not there, "he is up there, at a ranch of a *capo* named Nachito." Julio pointed to a rough dirt track that could be seen leading up into the mountains from

Tamazula.

On the way out of town and toward the mountains, Julio stopped and ducked into a tiny office to collect the monthly subsidy he receives from the Mexican government for not growing illegal drugs—despite the fact that he does grow opium and marijuana. This is another closely related contradiction and irony in Sinaloa, illustrating the "you leave me alone and I'll leave you alone" armistice that exists between the narcos and the government. A few minutes later, in the distance they spotted what appeared to be a platoon of soldiers. Julio suddenly decided that they should turn around and go back. He insisted that it would be unsafe to go any further. He argued that the armed men could be federal troops, El Chapo's men, *gatilleros* (triggermen) for the Beltran-Leyva cartel, or Zetas. In any case, they would recognize a *gringo* (American) in the car and assume that he was from the U.S. Drug Enforcement Agency (DEA) or U.S. Central Intelligence Agency (CIA). Julio was prickly and insistent: "If you want to find El Chapo, you should look near the village of La Tuna. I know people who can take you there."

On the way back to Culiacan, conversation stayed centered on the inordinately high level of violence and impunity to prosecution for it in Sinaloa. In the capital city, the front page of the newspaper now featured a street-by-street diagram of the most recent beheadings and assassinations: "El Mapa De La Muerte" (the death map).

Our reporter never did find out how the vendetta between El Chapo and Mochomo and Barbas came out. It really did not matter. The back and forth violence continues apace and seems to blur into a deep gray fog. In that fog, the violence between and within the rival cartels, the enforcer gangs, and government forces does not appear likely to end anytime soon. There is too much money to be made. In a lull in the almost ever-present self-enrichment process, a bunch of headless bodies—or just the heads—will be dropped somewhere conspicuous. And there may or may not be another note. Messages in Sinaloa no longer have to be written or explicit.

Conclusions.

The TCOs, their enforcer gangs, and the Zetas members operating in Sinaloa have marginalized Mexican state authority and replaced it with a criminal anarchy. That anarchy is defined by bribes, patronage, cronyism, violence, and personal whim. The present vision of the human capacity to treat automatic weapons' fire and the terrified screams of victims from "down the street" as mere background noise to the Sinaloa soap opera should create, at the least, a vague unease. A future vision of larger and larger parts of Mexico and the global community adapting to criminal values and forms of behavior should be, at a minimum, unsettling.

This cautionary tale of a significant criminal challenge to effective state sovereignty and traditional Western values takes us to the problem of response. Even though commercial enrichment remains the primary motive for TCO and Zeta challenges to state security and sovereignty in Mexico, the strategic architecture of the Zetas (organization, motive, practices, and policies) resembles that of a political or ideological insurgency. The primary objective of the political insurgents, drug cartels, and private armies such as the Zetas is to attain the level of freedom of movement and action that allows the achievement of the desired enrichment. This defines insurgency: that is, coercing radical change of a given political, economic, and social system in order to neutralize it, control it, or depose it. Rephrased slightly, it also defines war: that is, compelling an adversary to accede to an aggressor's policy objectives.[58]

By responding to this kind of challenge to security, stability, and sovereignty with a piecemeal and incoherent law enforcement approach or with an ad hoc and violent military approach, political leaders are playing into the hands of the cartels and TCO-gang phenomenon. Even worse, by condoning corrupt practices and hoping that the problem will go away, legitimate leaders are letting their adversaries play all the proverbial cards. Contemporary political, military, and opinion leaders must change their fundamental thought patterns (mindsets) and strengthen national and multilateral organizational structures in order to deal more effectively with this overwhelming reality.

RECOMMENDATIONS

Again, as stated above, the power to deal effectively with the kinds of threats posed by the gang-TCO phenomenon is not hard combat firepower or even the more benign police power. Power is multilevel and multilateral and combines political, psychological, moral, informational, economic, and social efforts— as well as police, military, and civil-bureaucratic activities — that can be brought to bear holistically on the causes and consequences, as well as the perpetrators, of violence. Ultimately, then, success in contemporary irregular conflict comes as a result of a unified effort to apply the full human and physical resources of a nation-state and its international partners to achieve the individual and collective well-being that leads to sustained societal peace with justice.

The actions, investments, and reforms needed to generate the kind of power that can address the macro-level strategic socioeconomic and police-military problems exacerbated by the gang-TCO phenomenon must come from the Mexican government and society. In the meantime, there is still much to be done. The United States, under the Merida Initiative, is providing a 3-year $1.4 billion aid package aimed at helping Mexico fight the drug cartels with increased law enforcement training, military equipment, and improved bilateral intelligence cooperation.[59] Even though more micro tactical-operational level aid will help, the fundamental question is whether the Mexican, U.S., and other interested governments will focus on the problem long enough to change the drug war paradigm from a micro to a macro approach.

A macro strategic and practical approach to the gang-TCO phenomenon must begin with a mindset change and the promulgation of a cognitive basis for effective change. That is, while a combination of law enforcement and military power is necessary to deal with the problem, it is insufficient. The key to greater success in this kind of irregular conflict is "a shift in emphasis toward thinking better and fighting smarter."[60] Accordingly, the author of this statement from a RAND Occasional Paper argues that there are two requirements to fighting smarter. They are to (1) create institutional conditions conducive to using brains more than bullets; and (2) implement measures designed to develop brain power and put it to good use.[61]

The first recommendation, then, requires the following:

- A flat (rather than traditional hierarchical)

organizational structure, with leadership cognitively prepared to coordinate and implement macro whole-of-government efforts to address the multifaceted and dynamic threat in a timely manner.

- That, in turn, requires professionalization and modernization of civilian-police-military leadership capable of identifying and meeting critical analytical, planning, operational, and strategic decisionmaking needs (for example, institutional reform and personnel investment) for a prioritized and balanced approach to the larger issues of Mexican and hemispheric security.

The second recommendation involves a serious investment in people and brain power. That would entail:

- Revising current personnel policies to recruit and promote individuals who demonstrate great intellectual aptitude for solving unfamiliar and ambiguous problems;
- Providing continuing professional education and training and bilateral personnel exchanges at all levels;
- Exploiting networks and networked information quickly and fully; and,
- Decentralizing authority to make decisions.[62]

These recommendations call for some organizational reform and serious investment in improving civil-police-military cognitive capacity. It is time to take the wisdom of Sun Tzu seriously. He left for posterity this exhortation from the opening of his famous *Art of War*: "War is a matter of vital importance to the State. The province of life or death; the road to survival or ruin. It is mandatory that it be thoroughly studied."[63]

ENDNOTES

1. Lincoln B. Krause, "The Guerrillas Next Door," *Low Intensity Conflict & Law Enforcement*, Spring 1999, pp. 34–56. Also see Jose Luis Velasco, *Insurgency, Authoritarianism, and Drug Trafficking in Mexico's Democratization*, New York: Routledge, 2005; and Max G. Manwaring, "Sovereignty under Siege: Gangs and Other Criminal Organizations in Central America and Mexico," in *Insurgency, Terrorism & Crime*, Norman: University of Oklahoma Press, 2008, pp. 104–128.

2. See note 1. Also see Mark Stevenson, "Commission says Central American Mara gangs have taken root in Mexico," *www.signonsandiago.com*, 4/4/2008; Alfredo Corchado and Laurence Iliff, "Ex-rivals merge to 'megacartel' intensifies brutality in Mexico," *www.dallasnews.com*, 7/9/2008; Ioan Grillo, "Behind Mexico's Wave of Beheadings," *www.time.com*, 1/22/2009; Ioan Grillo, "Confessions of a Mexican Narco Foot-Soldier," *www.time.com*, 1/22/2009; Robin Emmott, "Mexico's Gulf Cartel undaunted by military assault," *www.reuters.com*, 1/22/2009; and Tim Padgett, "The Killers Next Door," *www.time.com*, 1/22/2009.

3. Private armies are not new. They have been operating at one level or another for centuries, and John Sullivan cites data to the effect that "[s]everal hundred currently operate in over 100 nations, on six continents, generating over $100 billion in annual revenues." See John P. Sullivan, "Terrorism, Crime, and Private Armies," *Low Intensity Conflict & Law Enforcement*, Winter 2002, pp. 239–253.

4. James Rosenau, *Turbulence in World Politics*, Princeton, NJ: Princeton University Press, 1990. Also note that Mexico admits to 233 "Zones of Impunity"; see Marc Lacey, "In Drug War, Mexico Fights Cartels and Itself," *New York Times*, March 30, 2009, at *www.nytimes.com/2009/03/30/world/americas/30mexico.html*. Also see Peter W. Singer, "Peacekeepers, Inc.," *Policy Review*, June 2003.

5. See note 1. Also see author interview with the personal representative of the attorney general of Mexico in the United States, Dr. Manuel Suarez-Meir, in Washington, DC, January 29,

2009.

6. Sullivan, 2002, pp. 244–249.

7. This term comes from the title of Krause's article cited in note 1.

8. The methodology is taken from Robert K. Yin, *Case Study Research: Design and Methods*, Thousand Oaks, CA: Sage Publications, 1994, pp. 1–10, 15, 31–32, 140, and 147.

9. Charles Gibson, *Spain in America*, New York: Harper and Row, 1966; Hubert Herring, *A History of Latin America from the Beginnings to the Present*, New York: Knopf, 1968; Thomas E. Skidmore and Peter H. Smith, *Modern Latin America*, New York: Oxford University Press, 1984; and Frank Tannenbaum, *Ten Keys to Latin America*, New York: Knopf, 1962. Also see George W. Grayson, "Los Zetas: The Ruthless Army Spawned by a Mexican Drug Cartel," Washington, DC: Foreign Policy Research Institute, April 30, 2008; George W. Grayson, *Mexico's Struggle with "Drugs and Thugs,"* Washington, DC: Foreign Policy Association Headline Series, Winter 2009; Colleen W. Cook, "Mexico's Drug Cartels," *Congressional Research Service Report to Congress*, February 25, 2008, Order Code RL34215, hereafter cited as *CRS Report*; Machael Patrou, "Mexico's Civil War," *Maclean's*, December 8, 2008; and Sullivan, 2002, 239–253.

10. Robert E. Scott, *Mexican Government in Transition*, Urbana: University of Illinois Press, 1964; Roger D. Hanson, *The Politics of Mexican Development*, Baltimore, MD: Johns Hopkins University Press, 1971; Martin C. Needler, *Mexican Politics: The Containment of Conflict*, New York: Dragon, 1982; and Daniel Levy and Gabriel Szekelup, *Mexico: Paradoxes of Stability and Change*, Boulder, CO: Westview Press, 1983.

11. See notes 8 and 9.

12. Tannenbaum, 1962.

13. *Ibid.*; and note 9.

14. David C. Jordan, *Drug Politics*, Norman: University of

Oklahoma Press, 1999, pp. 19, 142–157.

15. Sullivan, 2002.

16. Jordan, 1999, p. 19.

17. *Ibid.* Also see Mark Stevenson, "Mexican Singer Slain in Hospital while Recovering from Gunshot Wounds," *www. signonsandiego.com*, 12/4/2007; Ana Arana, "How the Street Gangs Took Control of Central America," *Foreign Affairs,* May–June 2005, pp. 98–110; and John P. Sullivan, "Maras Morphing: Revisiting Third Generation Gangs," *Global Crime,* August–November 2006, pp. 488–490.

18. Jordan, 1999, pp. 142–157.

19. Sullivan, 2002, pp. 239–253. Also see Brian Jenkins, "Redefining the Enemy: The World Has Changed, But Our Mindset Has Not," *Rand Review*, Spring 2004.

20. Jordan, 1999, pp. 193–194.

21. *Ibid.*, p. 152. Also see Grayson, 2009; "Sinaloa Drug Cartel Said to Infiltrate Executive Branch," *Economic News & Analysis on Mexico*, *www.thefreelibrary.com*, 1/23/2009; Jane Bussey, "Organized Crime Takes Control in Parts of Mexico," McClatchy Washington Bureau, *www.mcclatchydc.com*, 9/20/2008; and "Reports: Cancun Police Chief Questioned in general's Killing," *www.cnn.com/2009/WORLD/americas*, 3/17/2009.

22. Phil Williams, *From the New Middle Ages to a New Dark Age: The Decline of the State and U.S. Strategy,* Carlisle, PA: Strategic Studies Institute, U.S. Army War College, 2008.

23. Sullivan, 2002, p. 239.

24. Chester A. Crocker, "Engaging Failed States," *Foreign Affairs*, September–October 2003, pp. 32–44; Steven D. Krasner and Carlos Pascual, "Addressing State Failure," *Foreign Affairs*, July–August 2005, pp. 153–155.

25. *CRS Report.* Also see "Central America and Mexico Gang

Assessment," Washington, DC: U.S. Agency for International Development, Bureau for Latin America and Caribbean Affairs, April 2006, hereafter cited as *AID Paper, 2006.*

26. W. Lee Rensselaer III, *The White Labyrinth,* New Brunswick, NJ: Transaction, 1990. Also see Max G. Manwaring, *Street Gangs: The New Urban Insurgency,* Carlisle, PA: Strategic Studies Institute, U.S. Army War College, 2005, p. 24.

27. See note 26. Also see Mark Stevenson, "Mexico: Drug Gangs Using Terror Tactics," *Miami Herald,* May 17, 2007, *www.miamiherald.com/915/story/110509.html.*

28. *Ibid.* Also see Kevin G. Hall, "Mexican Drug War Getting Bloodier," *Miami Herald,* March 21, 2007; and *AID Paper, 2006.*

29. See note 28. Also see statement of Chris Swecker, Assistant Director, Criminal Investigation Division, Federal Bureau of Investigation, before U.S. House of Representatives Committee on Judiciary, November 17, 2005, *www.fbi.gov/congress05/swecker111705.html,* 1/22/2009; "President Felipe Calderon Launches Ambitious Campaign against Drug Cartels," *Economic News & Analysis on Mexico,* January 24, 2007, *www.thefreelibrary.com,* 1/23/2009; and Oscar Becerra, "A to Z of Crime—Mexico's Zetas Expand Operations," *Jane's Intelligence Review,* January 30, 2009, *www.Z.janes.com/janesdata/maps/jir/history/jir2009...2/5/2009.*

30. See note 29. Also see Grayson, "Mexico and the Drug Cartels," August 17, 2007, *www.fpri.org;* and notes 2, 8, 23, and 24.

31. See note 30. Also see Williams, 2008.

32. Steven Metz and Raymond Millen, *Future Wars/Future Battlespace,* Carlisle, PA: Strategic Studies Institute, U.S. Army War College, 2003, pp. ix, 15–17.

33. Paul E. Smith, *On Political War,* Washington, DC: National Defense University Press, 1989, p. 3. Also see Carl von Clausewitz, *On War* [1832], Michael Howard and Peter Paret, trans. and eds., New Brunswick, NJ: Rutgers University Press, 1976, p. 75.

34. *Ibid.* Also see Jorge Verstrynge Rojas, *La guerra asimetrica y el Islam revolucionario (Asymmetric War and Revolutionary Islam),* Madrid, Spain: El Viejo Topo, 2005.

35. General Sir Frank Kitson, *Warfare as a Whole,* London: Faber and Faber, 1987. Also see General Sir Rupert Smith, *The Utility of Force: The Art of War in the Modern World,* New York: Alfred A. Knopf, 2007.

36. Carlos Marighella, *Manual of the Urban Guerrilla,* Chapel Hill, NC: Documentary Publications, 1985, p. 84.

37. *Ibid.*

38. *CRS Report,* pp. 4–5. Also see "Mexico's Civil War," *Maclean's,* December 8, 2008, pp. 24–25; and Grayson, 2008 and 2009.

39. Subdued debate regarding whether Mexico was or is moving toward failed state status was enlivened both in Mexico and the United States by General (Retired) Barry R. McCaffrey's presentation to Roger Rufe, entitled "A Strategic and Operational Assessment of Drugs and Crime in Mexico," dated March 16, 2009. See *www.brm@mccaffreyassociates.com.* Also note that Velasco, 2005, p. 2, states that Mexico's democracy is "partial, weak, contradictory, and superficial."

40. Grayson, 2008.

41. *CRS Report,* p. 11. Also see Martin Morita, "Desaten carteles guerra en el sureste" ("Separating Cartels and War in the Southeast"), *Reforma,* July 27, 2006.

42. Marighella, 1985. Also see Grayson, 2008. Also note that in response to Gulf Cartel initiatives, the rival Sinaloa Cartel has created its own enforcer gangs. The Negros and the Polones are less sophisticated and effective than the Zetas, but they appear to have little problem confronting local police and—of course—unprotected civilians. See Alfredo Corchado, "Cartel's Enforcers Outpower Their Boss," *Dallas Morning News,* June 11, 2007.

43. See note 43. Benetez is quoted in the Corchado article in the preceding note.

44. *AID Paper, 2006.*

45. Max G. Manwaring, "La soberania bajo asedio: Las Pandillas y otras organizaciones criminales en Centroamerica y en Mexico" ("Sovereignty Under Seige: Gangs and Other Criminal Organizations in Central America and Mexico"), *Air & Space Power Journal,* 2nd trimester 2008, pp. 25–41.

46. Alejanddro Suverza, "Los Zetas, una pasadilla para el cartel de Golfo" ("The Zetas, Two Faces for the Gulf Cartel"), *El Universal,* January 12, 2008; Oscar Becerra, "A to Z of Crime: Mexico's Zetas Expand Operations," *Jane's Intelligence Review,* January 30, 2009; and Grayson, 2008 and 2009.

47. *Ibid.*

48. *Economist,* March 7, 2009, pp. 30–33; and Marc Lacey, "With Deadly Persistence, Mexican Drug Cartels Get Their Way," *New York Times,* March 1, 2009, pp. 1, 9.

49. Becerra, 2009, pp. 1–9; and Grayson, 2008, p. 2.

50. Williams, 2008; and Phil Williams, *Mexican Futures,* unpublished monograph, n.d.

51. See note 51.

52. John P. Sullivan and Robert J. Bunker, "Drug Cartels, Street Gangs, and Warlords," in Robert J. Bunker, ed., *Nonstate Threats and Future Wars,* London: Frank Cass, 2003, pp. 45–53.

53. Robert J. Bunker and John P. Sullivan, "Cartel Evolution: Potentials and Consequences," *Transnational Organized Crime,* Summer 1998, pp. 55–74.

54. Sullivan, 2006, p. 501.

55. Peter Lupsha, "Grey Area Phenomenon: New Threats and Policy Dilemmas," unpublished paper presented at the High Intensity Crime/Low Intensity Conflict Conference, Chicago, IL, September 27–30, 1992, pp. 22–23.

56. The following vignette is taken from Guy Lawson, "The War Next Door," *Rolling Stone*, November 13, 2008.

57. Mark Stevenson, "Top Mexico Cops Charged with Favoring Drug Cartel," Associated Press, January 24, 2009, *www.news.yahoo.com*, 1/26/2009.

58. See, as an example, Clausewitz, [1832] 1976, p. 75.

59. Elise Lebott, "U.S. Puts Finishing Touches on Anti-Drug Effort with Mexico," CNN News, March 27, 2009, *www.CNN.com*.

60. David Gombert, *Heads We Win: The Cognitive Side of Counterinsurgency (COIN)*, Rand Occasional Paper, Santa Monica, CA: RAND National Defense Institute, 2007, pp. 35–56.

61. *Ibid.*

62. *Ibid.*

63. Sun Tzu, *The Art of War*, Samuel B. Griffiths, trans., London, United Kingdom: Oxford University Press, 1971, p. 63.

www.ingramcontent.com/pod-product-compliance
Lightning Source LLC
Chambersburg PA
CBHW081755280526

45789CB00008B/2871